Utah Unveiled

Your Ultimate Guide to Planning an Unforgettable Adventure and Scenic Trip Through the Beehive State's Natural Wonders and Cultural Treasures

Patricia T. Shay

UTAH TOURIST MAP

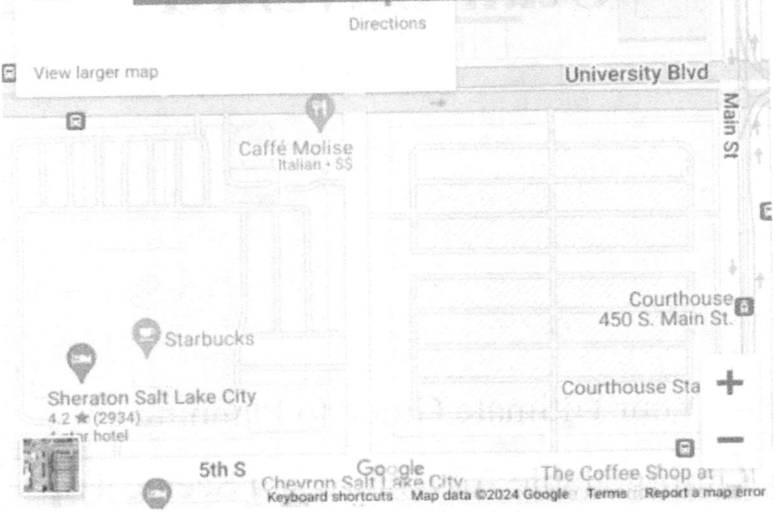

HOW TO SCAN THE QR CODE

- Open your camera app.
- Align the QR code.
- Wait for the prompt.
- Follow the link or action.
- Use a QR code scanner app if necessary

TABLE OF CONTENTS

Introduction

Overview of Utah

Colorado to the east, Wyoming to the northeast, Idaho to the north, Arizona to the south, and Nevada to the west are the states that provide Utah with its borders. Utah is situated in the western region of the United States. Arid deserts, lush woods, gorgeous mountains, and rare geological formations are just some of the features that may be found in the state's geography, which is immensely diversified. A large number of national parks and monuments in Utah showcase the state's varied topography, which has earned the state a reputation for its breathtaking natural beauty.

Principal Urban Areas

The biggest city in Utah and the capital of the state, Salt Lake City is particularly well-known for its historic Temple Square, its lively downtown, and its proximity to the Great Salt Lake.

Provo is the location of Brigham Young University, which provides a balanced combination of intellectual culture with the splendor of nature.

Ogden is famed for its extensive railroad heritage as well as its proximity to a variety of outdoor activities.

The city of St. George serves as the entrance to Zion National Park, which is famous for its pleasant environment and breathtaking red rock landscape.

Parks and Natural Wonders of the United States

The four national parks that make up Utah's "Mighty 5" are well-known.

a. **Arches National Park:** Famous for its approximately 2,000 natural stone arches.
b. **Bryce Canyon National Park:** Known for its unusual hoodoos and stunning panoramas.
c. **Canyonlands National Park:** Featuring magnificent canyons and buttes carved by the Colorado River.
d. **Capitol Reef National Park:** Known for its rough topography and the Waterpocket Fold.
e. **Zion National Park:** Famous for its high cliffs, tight valleys, and unique ecosystems.

Additionally, Monument Valley, Antelope Island State Park, and the Great Salt Lake are must-see natural features.

Climate Utah enjoys a semi-arid to arid climate, with major differences owing to its varied topography. Summers are often hot and dry, but winters may be chilly with heavy snowfall in mountainous locations, making Utah a popular destination for winter sports. Spring and autumn bring pleasant weather, suitable for outdoor activities.

Culture and History

Utah has a rich cultural legacy, impacted by Native American tribes, early pioneers, and Mormon immigrants. The state's history is inextricably connected with The Church of Jesus Christ of Latter-day Saints (LDS Church), which had a vital influence on colonization and growth.

Key cultural and historical sites include:

a. **Temple Square in Salt Lake City:** The spiritual and administrative hub of the LDS Church.
b. **Natural Heritage Museum of Utah:** Showcasing the state's natural and cultural heritage.

Ancestral Puebloan Sites: Such as the ancient cliff homes in southern Utah.

Outdoor Activities

Utah is a sanctuary for outdoor lovers, providing a broad choice of activities:

a. **Hiking & Backpacking:** From minor paths to multi-day excursions in national parks.
b. **Mountain Biking:** Especially popular in Moab with its world-class routes.
c. **Rock Climbing:** With notable places like Zion National Park and Indian Creek. **Water Sports:** Including boating, fishing, and paddleboarding on Utah's lakes and rivers.
d. **Winter Sports:** Skiing and snowboarding at famous resorts including Park City, Deer Valley, and Snowbird.

Utah's economy is varied, with significant industries including technology, tourism, mining, agriculture, and manufacturing. The state has undergone tremendous economic development in recent years, spurred by a rising tech sector frequently referred to as the "Silicon Slopes."

Demographics

Utah has a population of approximately 3 million people, with a young and quickly rising populace. The state is noted for its strong sense of community, good quality of life, and family-friendly atmosphere.

a. **Transportation Air Travel:** Salt Lake City International Airport is the principal hub, serving various domestic and international flights.
b. **Roads & roads:** Utah boasts a vast network of highways and picturesque byways, making it a great location for road excursions.
c. **Public Transport:** Includes light rail (TRAX), commuter rail (FrontRunner), and bus services, particularly in the Salt Lake City metropolitan region.

Utah is a place of outstanding natural beauty, rich cultural traditions, and boundless chances for adventure. Whether you're visiting its renowned national parks, diving into its history, or enjoying its lively towns, Utah provides something for every tourist.

Why Visit Utah

There are various compelling reasons to visit Utah, each showcasing its distinct attractiveness and attractions:

Natural Beauty and Landscapes

a. **National Parks:** Utah is home to five gorgeous national parks, each boasting distinctive landscapes including towering red rock formations, arches, canyons, and wide panoramas.

b. **Scenic Drives:** From the harsh landscape of Monument Valley to the stunning rock formations in Zion and Bryce Canyon, Utah's scenic drives are unrivaled.

c. **Diverse Geography:** Experience everything from snowy ranges to desert vistas and salt flats within a few hours' travel.

Outdoor Recreation

a. **Hiking and Backpacking:** Explore various routes that lead to secret arches, magnificent vistas, and isolated canyons.

b. **Rock Climbing:** Utah provides world-class climbing possibilities with sandstone cliffs and demanding routes.
c. **River Rafting:** Enjoy exhilarating whitewater excursions on the Colorado River and other gorgeous rivers.

Cultural and Historical Sites

a. **Native American Heritage:** Discover ancient rock art, cliff dwellings, and archeological sites that highlight Utah's rich Native American past.
b. **Pioneer History:** Visit historic landmarks like Temple Square in Salt Lake City and learn about Utah's Mormon pioneer legacy.

Events and Festivals

a. **Outdoor Festivals:** Experience events like the Sundance Film Festival in Park City, famed for its independent films and mountain location.
b. **Arts & Culture:** Utah has several arts festivals, music performances, and cultural events throughout the year.

Family-Friendly Activities

a. **Theme Parks:** Enjoy family fun at Lagoon Amusement Park in Salt Lake City.
b. **Wildlife Viewing:** Visit Hogle Zoo and Tracy Aviary in Salt Lake City, or explore Antelope Island State Park for bison and birding.

Winter Sports

a. **Skiing & Snowboarding:** Utah's ski resorts are noted for their copious snowfall, steep terrain, and convenient accessibility from Salt Lake City.
b. **Snowshoeing & Cross-Country Skiing:** Explore beautiful winter landscapes in national forests and state parks.

Culinary Delights

a. **Local Cuisine:** Experience Utah's culinary culture, from local brewpubs and farm-to-table restaurants to southwestern cuisine and regional delicacies.

Whether you're an outdoor enthusiast, historical buff, cultural adventurer, or just seeking natural beauty, Utah provides a multitude of events that appeal to every interest and season.

Best Time to Visit

Utah is a year-round destination, with each season bringing distinct experiences and attractions. The optimal time to visit depends on your interests and the activities you want to conduct.

Spring (March to May)

a. **Pros:**

Mild weather and flowering wildflowers.

Ideal for hiking, biking, and touring national parks.

Fewer crowds compared to summer.

b. **Cons:**

Weather may be erratic, with occasional rain and snow in higher altitudes.

c. **Highlights:**

Arches and Canyonlands National Parks are gorgeous with fewer visitors.

Zion National Park provides great hiking conditions.

Annual activities include the Moab Jeep Safari and the Utah Arts Festival.

Summer (June to August)

a. **Pros:**

Warm weather and lengthy days are great for outdoor excursions.

Festivals and festivities are in full swing.

Great for water sports in lakes and reservoirs.

b. **Cons:**

High temperatures, particularly in arid places like Moab and Zion.

Crowds at renowned national parks and tourist destinations.

Higher accommodation rates.

c. **Highlights:**

Lake Powell and the Great Salt Lake are perfect for boating and swimming.

Cooler mountain areas like Park City and the Uintas provide a reprieve from the heat.

Summer concerts, outdoor theater, and the Utah Shakespeare Festival.

Fall (September to November)

a. **Pros:**

Cooler temps and gorgeous autumn foliage.

Fewer crowds than in summer.

Ideal for hiking, bicycling, and picturesque driving.

b. **Cons:**

Shorter daylight hours.

Some alpine regions may start to get early snowfall.

c. **Highlights:**

Spectacular autumn colors in locations like the Wasatch Range and Zion National Park.

Harvest festivals and farmers' markets.

Perfect time for visiting Bryce Canyon and Capitol Reef National Parks.

Winter (December to February)

a. **Pros:**

Excellent skiing and snowboarding in world-class destinations.

Fewer visitors in national parks, affording seclusion and distinctive winter scenery.

Holiday celebrations and events.

b. **Cons:**

Cold temps and snow in several regions.

Some roads and paths may be impassable due to snow.

c. **Highlights:**

Skiing and snowboarding at Park City, Deer Valley, Snowbird, and Alta.

Winter hiking and snowshoeing in areas like Bryce Canyon and Zion.

Sundance Film Festival in Park City.

Overall Recommendations

a. **Best for National Parks:** Spring and October provide the finest circumstances for exploring Utah's national parks with good weather and fewer visitors.

b. **Best for Skiing:** Winter is great for skiing and snowboarding in Utah's famous resorts.

c. **Best for Festivals & Events:** Summer and winter are prime periods for cultural festivals and activities.

When arranging your vacation, consider the exact things you wish to undertake and the weather conditions that suit you best. Each season in Utah has its charm and set of attractions, making it an adaptable destination for vacationers.

Chapter One: Exploring Salt Lake City

Attractions

Temple Square

a. **Description:** The spiritual heart of The Church of Jesus Christ of Latter-day Saints, boasts landmark structures and wonderfully manicured grounds.
b. **Highlights:** Salt Lake Temple, Tabernacle, Assembly Hall, and the reflecting pool.
c. **Activities:** Guided tours, organ performances, and learning about Mormon history and culture.

Utah State Capitol

a. **Description:** A beautiful architectural landmark overlooking the city.
b. **Highlights:** Capitol Hill, the Rotunda, and panoramic views of Salt Lake Valley.
c. **Activities:** Guided tours to learn about Utah's government and history.

Liberty Park

a. **Description:** Salt Lake City's oldest and most renowned park, including wide-open spaces, ponds, playgrounds, and picnic places.
b. **Highlights:** Tracy Aviary, with a wide array of birds, and Liberty Park Lake for paddle boating.
c. **Activities:** Walking, jogging, picnics, and enjoying outdoor activities.

The Leonardo Museum

a. **Description:** A modern museum examining the interface of science, technology, and art.
b. **Highlights:** Interactive exhibitions, changing art displays, and intriguing workshops.
c. **Activities:** Hands-on activities in fields including robotics, virtual reality, and creative expression.

Hogle Zoo

a. **Description:** A renowned zoological park presenting animals from throughout the globe in realistic environments.
b. **Highlights:** African savannah, Asian highlands, and the Rocky Shores aquatic display.

c. **Activities:** Zookeeper lectures, animal interactions, and seasonal activities.

Red Butte Garden and Arboretum

a. **Description:** A botanical garden containing different plant collections, themed gardens, and picturesque hiking routes.
b. **Highlights:** Outdoor performances at the Red Butte Garden Amphitheatre and seasonal plant sales.
c. **Activities:** Walking tours, birding, and visiting themed garden sections.

Tracy Aviary

a. **Description:** Located inside Liberty Park, this aviary is home to a broad range of birds from throughout the globe.
b. **Highlights:** Interactive bird exhibitions, bird shows, and educational events.
c. **Activities:** Bird viewing, photography, and learning about conservation activities.

These attractions provide a combination of cultural discovery, outdoor recreation, and educational activities, making Salt Lake City a fascinating destination for tourists of all ages and interests.

Dining and Nightlife

In Salt Lake City, you'll discover a range of food choices ranging from informal cafes to fine dining venues. Here are some top recommendations for food and nightlife in the city:

Dining Red Iguana

a. **Cuisine:** Authentic Mexican
b. **Highlights:** Known for its mole sauces and delicious foods. Try their famed moles and traditional Mexican meals.

Takashi

a. **Cuisine:** Japanese
b. **Highlights:** Offers sushi and other Japanese meals with a unique touch. Known for its high-quality fish and unique taste combinations.

The Copper Onion

a. **Cuisine:** New American

b. **Highlights:** Seasonal dinners incorporating locally sourced foods. Known for their charcuterie, burgers, and hefty main meals.

Squatters Pub Brewery

a. **Cuisine:** American, Brewery
b. **Highlights:** A neighborhood favorite for artisan beer and pub cuisine. Try their burgers, fish tacos, and seasonal beers.

Pago

a. **Cuisine:** Farm-to-table, Contemporary American
b. **Highlights:** Emphasizes locally sourced foods in their seasonal meals. Known for its inventive cuisine and handmade beverages.

Nightlife Bar X

a. **Description:** Classic cocktail bar with a relaxing vibe and a historic location.
b. **Highlights:** Craft drinks and a friendly setting. Perfect for a laid-back evening.

Lake Effect

a. **Description:** A bustling pub and music venue with a big range of creative drinks and beers.
b. **Highlights:** Live music events, DJs, and a huge outdoor terrace.

The Bayou

a. **Description:** A pub and restaurant noted for its large assortment of specialty beers and Cajun-inspired food.
b. **Highlights:** Over 300 kinds of beer, including rare and local beers. Live music on weekends adds to the dynamic atmosphere.

Twist

a. **Description:** Upscale bar and nightclub featuring beverages and DJ music.
b. **Highlights:** Rooftop terrace with views of downtown Salt Lake City. Known for its elegant ambiance and vibrant nightlife scene.

Gracie's

a. **Description:** A historic tavern and restaurant with a broad cuisine and a warm environment.
b. **Highlights:** Live music events, karaoke nights, and a huge outside terrace. Perfect for a casual night out with friends.

Whether you want to enjoy a gourmet dinner, sample local beers, or dance the night away, Salt Lake City provides eating and nightlife choices to fit every taste and inclination.

Events and Festivals

Salt Lake City holds several events and festivals throughout the year, exhibiting its ethnic diversity, outdoor lifestyle, and lively community spirit. Here are some prominent events and festivals to watch out for:

Events & Festivals in Salt Lake City Utah Arts Festival

a. **Description:** A major festival showcasing visual and performing arts, with live music, dance performances, art displays, and culinary arts.
b. **Location:** Library Square, downtown Salt Lake City.

c. **Timing:** Usually held in late June.

Sundance Film Festival

a. **Description:** One of the biggest independent film festivals in the United States, featuring a varied selection of films from across the globe.
b. **Location:** Various locations in Park City, Salt Lake City, and Sundance Mountain Resort.
c. **Timing:** Typically held in late January to early February.

Days of the '47 Parade and Rodeo

a. **Description:** Commemorates Utah's pioneer legacy with a parade involving floats, music, and horse entries. The associated rodeo celebrates Western culture with bull riding, barrel racing, and more.
b. **Location:** Downtown Salt Lake City.
c. **Timing:** Parade on July 24th (Pioneer Day), rodeo festivities at the same time.

Twilight Concert Series

a. **Description:** A summer concert series featuring nationally and globally famous artists playing in downtown Salt Lake City.
b. **Location:** Gallivan Center, downtown Salt Lake City.
c. **Timing:** Held on Thursday nights from July to August.

Utah State Fair

a. **Description:** A conventional state fair includes agricultural displays, amusement attractions, live entertainment, and a variety of food vendors.
b. **Location:** Utah State Fairpark, Salt Lake City.
c. **Timing:** Usually held in early September.

Downtown Farmers Market

a. **Description:** A weekly market exhibiting local vegetables, handmade crafts, food vendors, and live music.
b. **Location:** Pioneer Park, downtown Salt Lake City.
c. **Timing:** Held on Saturdays from June to October, then on Tuesdays from August to October.

Outdoor Retailer Snow Show

a. **Description:** An industry trade exhibition featuring the newest in outdoor gear, clothes, and equipment for winter sports and outdoor enjoyment.
b. **Location:** Salt Palace Convention Center, in Salt Lake City.
c. **Timing:** Typically held in late January.

These events and festivals look at Salt Lake City's dynamic cultural scene, outdoor lifestyle, and community festivities throughout the year. Whether you're interested in arts and culture, outdoor activities, or just appreciating local customs, there's something for everyone to enjoy in Salt Lake City's event calendar.

Chapter Two: Exploring Moab

Arches National Park

Arches National Park, situated near Moab in southwestern Utah, is famed for its beautiful natural stone arches and other geological structures formed by millions of years of erosion. Here's all you need to know to tour this historic park:

Overview

a. **Location:** Near Moab, Utah, accessible via US Route 191.
b. **Natural Features:** Over 2,000 natural stone arches, towering pinnacles, fins, and balancing rocks.
c. **Geological Significance:** Formed by erosion and weathering of Entrada Sandstone over millions of years.
d. **Environment:** Arid desert environment with scorching summers and freezing winters; spring and autumn are great for visiting.

Key Attractions

Delicate Arch

a. **Description:** The iconic freestanding arch symbolizes Utah.
b. **Hike:** Delicate Arch Trail (3 miles round trip); somewhat tough but gives great vistas.

Landscape Arch

a. **Description:** Longest natural arch in North America.
b. **Hike:** Easy 1.6-mile round trek from the Devil's Garden Trailhead.

Balanced Rock

a. **Description:** Giant sandstone boulder perched on a small pedestal.
b. **Viewpoint:** Visible from the road; short hike to its base.

Activities

a. **Hiking:** Trails vary from short walks to strenuous treks. Besides Delicate Arch and Landscape Arch, treks like Double Arch and Fiery Furnace provide unique experiences.

b. **Scenic Drives:** Arches Scenic Drive gives access to vistas and trailheads. Some locations are accessible exclusively by four-wheel drive vehicles.

c. **Photography**: Sunrise and dusk give great lighting for shooting the park's rich hues and structures.

d. **Stargazing:** Designated as an International Dark Sky Park; gives exceptional opportunity fcr seeing stars and Milky Way.

Visitor Information

a. **Entrance Fees:** Required; visit the National Park Service website for current costs.

b. **Visitor Center:** Located near the park entrance; includes displays, maps, and information on trails and safety.

c. **Best Time to Visit:** Spring and autumn for pleasant weather and fewer visitors; summer may be hot, while winter may bring snowfall.

Arches National Park provides a strange environment and amazing experiences, making it a must-visit location for nature enthusiasts and photographers alike.

Canyonlands National Park

Canyonlands National Park, situated near Moab in southwestern Utah, is a huge wilderness of canyons, mesas, and buttes sculpted by the Colorado River and its tributaries. Here's a guide to explore this tough and gorgeous park:

Overview

a. **Location:** Near Moab, Utah; separated into four districts: Island in the Sky, The Needles, The Maze, and the rivers.
b. **Natural Features:** Dramatic landscapes formed by millions of years of erosion, including deep canyons, towering spires, and mesas.
c. **Geological Significance:** Features rock strata going back over 300 million years.
d. **Environment:** Arid desert environment with scorching summers and freezing winters; spring and autumn are great for visiting.

Key Attractions by District Island in the Sky

a. **Description:** The most accessible region with magnificent views of canyons and rivers.
b. **Highlights:** Grand View Point Overlook, Mesa Arch, and Upheaval Dome (geological feature).
c. **Activities:** Scenic drives (Island in the Sky Scenic Drive), hiking (including short treks to views).

The Needles

a. **Description:** Known for its beautiful rock pinnacles (needles) and inaccessible backcountry treks.
b. **Highlights:** Chesler Park, Joint Trail, and Elephant Hill (difficult four-wheel-drive road).
c. **Activities:** Backpacking, hiking (Chesler Park Loop), and beautiful driving (Needles Overlook).

The Maze

a. **Description:** Remote and mountainous territory accessible only by high-clearance vehicles.
b. **Highlights:** Maze Overlook, Doll House (rock formations), and Maze District Petroglyphs.

c. **Activities:** Backcountry camping, four-wheel drive (Hans Flat Ranger Station access), and multi-day treks.

Rivers

a. **Description:** Includes the Green and Colorado Rivers, which form steep gorges across the park.
b. **Highlights:** White Rim Road (scenic driving and mountain riding), and river rafting.
c. **Activities:** Rafting tours (permission necessary), fishing, and visiting river viewpoints.

Activities

a. **Hiking:** Trails vary from short walks to hard treks, giving different scenery and vistas.
b. **Beautiful roads:** Each area includes beautiful roads with views and access to trailheads.
c. **Photography:** Sunrise and dusk give wonderful lighting for shooting the park's magnificent scenery.
d. **Stargazing:** Designated as an International Dark Sky Park; provides exceptional chances for stargazing.

Visitor Information

a. **Entrance Fees:** Required; visit the National Park Service website for current costs.

b. **Visitor Centers:** Located throughout each district (excluding The Maze); give information, exhibitions, and maps.

c. **Best Time to Visit:** Spring and autumn for pleasant weather and fewer visitors; summer may be hot, while winter may bring snowfall.

Canyonlands National Park provides explorers and nature lovers an opportunity to explore some of the most difficult and spectacular environments in the American Southwest. Whether you're climbing legendary arches, driving through panoramic panoramas, or camping under a starry sky, Canyonlands delivers an amazing outdoor experience.

Outdoor Activities and Local Eats

Moab, Utah, is a paradise for outdoor lovers, providing a broad selection of activities among its magnificent red rock scenery. Here's a guide to some of the greatest outdoor experiences you can do in Moab:

Hiking Arches National Park

a. **Highlights:** Delicate Arch, Landscape Arch, and Balanced Rock.
b. **Details:** Trails vary from simple to hard, giving famous arches and panoramic vistas.

Canyonlands National Park

a. **Highlights:** Mesa Arch, Grand View Point, and Chesler Park.
b. **Details:** Diverse pathways traverse deep valleys and high mesas, varied in difficulty.

Dead Horse Point State Park

a. **Highlights:** Dead Horse Point Overlook and hiking paths around the rim.
b. **Details:** Scenic walks affording amazing views of the Colorado River and Canyonlands.

Mountain Biking Slickrock Trail

a. **Details:** Famous for its rugged terrain and spectacular views of the Colorado River.
b. **Tip:** Best handled in colder months owing to its exposed aspect.

Klondike Bluffs

a. **Details:** Offers various routes through slick rock and sandstone formations.
b. **Tip:** Varied paths are ideal for various ability levels, with stunning viewpoints.

Rock Climbing Indian Creek

a. **Details:** Renowned for its world-class crack climbing routes.
b. **Tip:** Requires a permit and proper gear; good for experienced climbers.

Fisher Towers

a. **Details:** Iconic towers with pathways for all skill levels.
b. **Tip:** Guided excursions offered for beginners; beautiful views of the Colorado River.

Local Eats in Moab

Moab provides a range of eating alternatives, from informal cafes to gourmet dining locations. Here are some local favorites to try:

Eklecticafe

a. **Cuisine:** Breakfast and brunch
b. **Highlights:** Creative omelets, breakfast burritos, and fresh smoothies.

The Moab Brewery

a. **Cuisine:** American, brewery
b. **Highlights:** Handcrafted brews and pub cuisine including burgers, sandwiches, and pizzas.

Milt's Stop & Eat

a. **Cuisine:** Burgers with fries
b. **Highlights:** Classic roadside restaurant famed for its superb burgers and milkshakes.

Sunset Grill

a. **Cuisine:** American, fine dining

b. **Highlights:** Spectacular views of Moab and the surrounding red cliffs; cuisine comprises steaks, seafood, and pasta dishes.

Sweet Cravings Bakery + Bistro

a. **Cuisine:** Bakery, bistro

b. **Highlights:** Freshly baked products, sandwiches, salads, and specialty coffee.

Tips for Outdoor Activities

a. **Weather:** Check predictions and schedule activities appropriately; summers may be scorching, while winters may offer colder temps.

b. **Permissions:** Some activities like wilderness hiking or rock climbing may need permissions; check with local authorities.

c. **Safety:** Stay hydrated, use proper gear, and respect park restrictions and animals.

Moab's unique combination of outdoor experiences and local cuisine makes it a must-visit destination for nature lovers and culinary fans alike. Whether you're touring historic national parks or enjoying delectable food, Moab guarantees an amazing experience in the heart of Utah's red rock country.

Chapter Three: Exploring Park City

Ski Resorts

Park City, Utah, is recognized for its great ski resorts, providing world-class slopes, magnificent mountain vistas, and a variety of winter activities. Here are the main ski resorts you can discover in and near Park City:

Top Ski Resorts in Park City Park City Mountain Resort

- ✓ **Description:** One of the biggest ski resorts in the United States, recognized for its huge terrain and various lines.
- ✓ **Highlights:** Over 7,300 acres of skiable terrain, 17 peaks, and a variety of slopes for all ability levels.
- ✓ **Activities:** Skiing, snowboarding, snowshoeing, snow tubing, and picturesque gondola rides.
- ✓ **Tip:** Check out the Alpine Coaster and Flying Eagle Zipline for further experiences.

Deer Valley Resort

- ✓ **Description:** A premium resort noted for its expensive facilities and great customer service.

- ✓ **Highlights:** Impeccably groomed slopes, excellent eating choices, and luxury hotels.
- ✓ **Activities:** Skiing (no snowboarding permitted), snowshoeing, cross-country skiing, and exquisite dining at on-mountain lodges.
- ✓ **Tip:** Deer Valley restricts the number of skiers each day to optimize the tourist experience.

Canyons Village at Park City

- ✓ **Description:** Part of Park City Mountain Resort, giving a unique base area with its services and rooms.
- ✓ **Highlights:** Expansive terrain with a broad choice of ski tracks, from beginning slopes to demanding runs.
- ✓ **Activities:** Skiing, snowboarding, snowshoeing, eating, and après-ski entertainment.
- ✓ **Tip:** Explore the colorful town scene with stores, restaurants, and après-ski alternatives.

Additional Tips for Skiing in Park City

- ✓ **Lift Tickets**: Purchase tickets in advance to receive the cheapest pricing and avoid lengthy lineups.

- ✓ **Equipment Rental:** Numerous rental shops provide high-quality gear, including choices for skis, snowboards, boots, and helmets.
- ✓ **Lessons:** Whether you're a novice or want to enhance your skills, ski lessons are offered for all ages and levels.
- ✓ **Off-Piste Activities:** Explore neighboring activities like ice skating, dog sledding, and snowmobiling for more winter fun.

Park City's ski resorts provide not only outstanding winter sports activities but also magnificent lodgings, eating, and entertainment choices, making it a top destination for skiing fans from across the globe.

Summer Activities

In Park City, Utah, summer throws up a whole new assortment of outdoor activities in its gorgeous mountain environment. Here are some excellent summer things to enjoy in Park City:

Summer Activities in Park City Mountain Biking

- ✓ **Description:** Park City is recognized for its wide network of mountain bike routes, catering to all ability levels.
- ✓ **Highlights:** Deer Valley Resort and Park City Mountain Resort provide lift-served mountain riding tracks with magnificent vistas.
- ✓ Tip: Rent bikes and gear from local businesses and explore paths like the Mid Mountain Trail or Wasatch Crest Trail.

Hiking

- ✓ **Description:** Explore picturesque paths that traverse through alpine meadows, aspen groves, and steep mountain terrain.
- ✓ **Highlights:** Summit Park paths, Armstrong Trail, and Guardsman Pass provide varied degrees of difficulty and spectacular panoramas.
- ✓ **Tip:** Carry lots of water, wear sturdy shoes, and verify trail conditions before venturing out.

Scenic Chairlift Rides

- ✓ **Description:** Enjoy panoramic views of the Wasatch Mountains without the hike.
- ✓ **Highlights:** Park City Mountain Resort and Deer Valley Resort provide chairlift rides with access to hiking trails, picnic sites, and picture possibilities.
- ✓ **Tip:** Sunset chairlift rides give spectacular vistas and a great experience.

Outdoor Concerts and Festivals

- ✓ **Description:** Park City presents a variety of outdoor concerts and events during the summer months.
- ✓ **Highlights:** Deer Valley Music Festival, Park City Kimball Arts Festival, and outdoor music at different locations.
- ✓ **Tip:** Check local event calendars for schedules and ticket information.

Fly Fishing

- ✓ **Description:** Experience world-class fly fishing on the Provo River and other adjacent streams and lakes.

- ✓ **Highlights:** Guided fishing expeditions give possibilities to capture trout among quiet mountain settings.
- ✓ **Tip:** Obtain a fishing license and hire a local guide for the greatest experience.

Golfing

- ✓ **Description:** Park City features numerous championship golf courses in scenic settings.
- ✓ **Highlights:** Park City Golf Club, Canyons Golf, and Soldier Hollow Golf Course provide difficult courses with magnificent mountain vistas.
- ✓ **Tip:** Book tee times in advance and enjoy eating choices at clubhouses.

Historic Main Street

- ✓ **Description:** Explore Park City's lovely historic area with its galleries, shops, and eateries.
- ✓ **Highlights:** Park City Museum, art galleries, and local stores provide an insight into the town's mining heritage and active cultural community.
- ✓ **Tip:** Take a historic walking tour or enjoy alfresco eating on Main Street.

Tips for Summer Activities

- ✓ **Weather:** Summer temperatures might fluctuate; take clothes and sunscreen.
- ✓ **Reservations:** Book activities and lodgings in advance, particularly during the high season.
- ✓ **Safety:** Stay hydrated, practice trail etiquette, and be alert to animals.

Park City's summer activities provide something for everyone, whether you're seeking adventure on the trails, relaxation among beautiful beauty, or cultural events in town. Enjoy visiting this mountain beauty during the warmer months!

Historic Main Street

Park City's Historic Main Street is a lovely and active neighborhood located within the magnificent Wasatch Mountains. Here's a guide to explore this historic area:

Overview

- ✓ **Location:** Downtown Park City, accessible from State Route 224.

- ✓ **Description:** A well-preserved mining town converted into a cultural hotspot, lined with Victorian buildings holding stores, galleries, restaurants, and pubs.
- ✓ **Historical Significance:** Originally a silver mining town in the 19th century, today a National old District featuring a combination of old buildings and contemporary facilities.

Things to Do Park City Museum

- ✓ **Description:** Located in the historic City Hall building, presenting exhibits on Park City's mining history, skiing tradition, and local culture.
- ✓ **Highlights:** Interactive exhibitions, relics, and guided tours offering insights into the town's development.

Art Galleries

- ✓ **Description:** Numerous galleries displaying local and international artists, covering a range of media including paintings, sculptures, and photography.

- ✓ **Highlights:** Kimball Art Center, Gallery MAR, and Meyer Gallery provide various collections and regularly hold exhibits and activities.

Shopping

- ✓ **Description:** Boutique shops and specialized boutiques selling unusual gifts, fashion, jewelry, and outdoor gear.
- ✓ **Highlights:** Dolly's Bookstore, Olive & Tweed, and Burns Cowboy Shop give a choice of shopping opportunities.

Dining and Nightlife

- ✓ **Description:** A gastronomic attraction featuring restaurants, cafés, and pubs catering to varied tastes.
- ✓ **Highlights:** High West Distillery & Saloon, Riverhorse on Main, and Handle provide gourmet meals and creative drinks in historic surroundings.

Outdoor Dining and Events

- ✓ **Description:** Sidewalk cafés and outdoor sitting spaces for enjoying meals and people-watching.

- ✓ **Highlights:** Summer outdoor concerts, art festivals, and the Sundance Film Festival contribute to the dynamic environment.

Tips for Visiting

- ✓ **Parking:** Use public parking places or street parking; consider walking or utilizing the free municipal transportation system.
- ✓ **Events:** Check local event calendars for festivals, art walks, and live music performances.
- ✓ **Hours:** Shops and galleries may have variable working hours; plan appropriately for meals and shopping.

Park City's Historic Main Street provides a lovely combination of history, culture, shopping, eating, and entertainment, making it a must-visit destination for visitors and residents alike. Whether you're touring its museums, perusing art galleries, or enjoying local food, the charm and character of Main Street Park City are guaranteed to make a lasting impression.

Chapter Four: Zion National Park

Hiking Trails

Zion National Park provides a range of hiking paths that display its spectacular scenery, from towering cliffs to verdant canyons and tumbling waterfalls. Here are some of the great hiking paths to explore:

The Narrows Description:

A renowned slot canyon walks where you wade into the Virgin River.

- **Length:** Variable (up to 16 miles round trip if hiking top-down).
- **Highlights:** Spectacular thin walls, hanging gardens, and distinctive rock formations.
- **Tip:** Rent water shoes and a walking stick from local outfitters for comfort and safety.

Angels Landing

- **Description:** A hard trek with exposed cliffs and spectacular panoramic vistas.
- **Length:** 5.4 kilometers round trip.

- **Highlights:** Scout Lookout, Walter's Wiggles (switchbacks), and stunning vistas from Angels Landing.
- **Tip:** Start early to avoid crowds and be prepared for steep drop-offs and restricted trails.

The Subway

- **Description:** A hard wilderness walks via a remarkable subway-shaped slot canyon.
- **Length:** 9.5 kilometers round trip.
- **Highlights:** Natural arches, waterfalls, and swimming holes in a lovely location.
- **Tip:** Requires a permit; technical canyoneering abilities may be essential at certain portions.

Emerald Pools

- **Description:** A family-friendly trek with three path alternatives leading to tranquil pools and waterfalls.
- **Length:** 1.2 to 3 kilometers round trip (depending on the path picked).
- **Highlights:** Lower, Middle, and Upper Emerald Pools with flowing waterfalls and rich greenery.

Tip: Best during spring for peak waterfall flow; beware of slick rocks.

Observation Point

- **Description:** A difficult trek giving panoramic views of Zion Canyon and beyond.
- **Length:** 8 kilometers round trip.
- **Highlights:** Echo Canyon, spectacular panoramas from Observation Point, and fewer people compared to Angels Landing.
- **Tip:** Start early and pack lots of water; affords a bird's-eye perspective of Angels Landing.

Tips for Hiking in Zion National Park:

- **Permits:** Some routes, including The Narrows and The Subway, need permits; get them in advance.
- **Safety:** Check weather conditions, bring lots of water, and wear sturdy shoes with adequate grip.
- **Crowds:** Start early or walk at off-peak hours to minimize congestion, particularly on famous routes like Angels Landing.

Zion National Park's hiking paths provide experiences ranging from peaceful strolls to difficult expeditions, each displaying the park's spectacular grandeur and natural treasures. Choose your path according to your fitness level, hobbies, and the time you have available to explore this amazing environment.

Scenic Drives

Exploring Zion National Park by automobile gives stunning views of its towering cliffs, verdant valleys, and various landscapes. Here are some lovely drives you shouldn't miss:

Zion Canyon Scenic Drive

- **Description:** A 6-mile trek in Zion Canyon, following the Virgin River.
- **Highlights:** Court of the Patriarchs, Weeping Rock, and multiple vistas.
- **Tip:** During peak season (March to November), entry is limited to shuttles; plan appropriately.

Zion-Mount Carmel Highway

- **Description:** Connects Zion Canyon to the east entrance of the park at Mount Carmel Junction.

- **Highlights:** Checkerboard Mesa, legendary switchbacks (known as the Zion-Mount Carmel Tunnel), and spectacular vistas of the canyonlands.
- **Tip:** Check for vehicle size limitations for the Zion-Mount Carmel Tunnel; bigger cars may need an escort.

Kolob Canyons Scenic Drive

- **Description:** Located in the northwest part of Zion National Park.
- **Highlights:** Panoramic vistas of red rock canyons, Kolob Arch (viewable from a distance), and picturesque viewpoints.
- **Tip:** Limited services; suitable for those wanting a peaceful experience away from the main canyon.

Tips for Scenic Drives:

- **Timing:** Early morning or late afternoon gives the finest light for shooting and fewer people.
- **Shuttle System:** During peak seasons, utilize the park's shuttle system for access to Zion Canyon Scenic Drive.

- **Safety:** Watch for animals on the roads and follow speed limits; stop over at authorized spots for photography.

Exploring Zion National Park by automobile enables you to experience its grandeur and different landscapes from the comfort of your vehicle, with several chances to stop, take photographs, and immerse yourself in the natural splendor of this renowned park.

Nearby Attractions

When visiting Zion National Park, there are various surrounding sights and areas of interest worth seeing outside the park limits. Here are some prominent sites you may visit:

Nearby Attractions from Zion National Park and Bryce Canyon National Park

- **Distance:** Approximately 72 miles northeast of Zion National Park.
- **Description:** Known for its unusual hoodoos (rock spires) and magnificent amphitheaters.

- **Highlights:** Bryce Amphitheater, Sunrise Point, Sunset Point, and hiking routes including Navajo Loop and Queens Garden.
- **Tip:** Plan for a day excursion to explore this strange environment of orange and pink rock formations.

Grand Staircase-Escalante National Monument

- **Distance:** Adjacent to Bryce Canyon, accessible by roads such as Highway 12.
- **Description:** A large and rough terrain with canyons, cliffs, and distinctive geological formations.
- **Highlights:** Slot gorges including Peek-a-Boo and Spooky Gulch, Escalante River, and gorgeous drives along Hole-in-the-Rock Road.
- **Tip:** Suitable for trekking, photography, and exploring distant nature locations.

Cedar Breaks National Monument

- **Distance:** Approximately 60 miles northwest of Zion National Park.
- **Description:** A natural amphitheater with colorful rock formations and vivid wildflowers.

- **Highlights:** Spectacular views from Point Supreme Overlook, Alpine Pond Trail, and the annual wildflower bloom (July to September).
- **Tip:** Visit during the summer months when the monument is accessible by automobile.

Capitol Reef National Park

- **Distance:** About 110 miles east of Zion National Park.
- **Description:** Known for its Waterpocket Fold, a geologic monocline stretching approximately 100 miles.
- **Highlights:** Scenic trip along Highway 24, Capitol Gorge Trail, Hickman Bridge, and ancient Fruita orchards.
- **Tip:** Explore the park's various landscapes, including canyons, cliffs, and petroglyphs.

Kolob Canyons

- **Distance:** Part of Zion National Park, reached by Interstate 15 near Cedar City.
- **Description:** Offers amazing views of red rock canyons and beautiful viewpoints.

- **Highlights:** Taylor Creek Trail, Kolob Arch (viewable from a distance), and calmer paths compared to the main canyon.
- **Tip:** Limited services; good for people seeking quiet and spectacular landscapes.

Tips for Exploring Nearby Attractions:

- **Plan Ahead:** Check weather conditions and road restrictions, particularly in rural locations.
- **Permissions:** Some activities like hiking in slot canyons or remote locations may need permissions; secure them in advance.
- **Time Management:** Allocate ample time to properly appreciate each trip; consider overnight stays for lengthy journeys.

Exploring these local sites from Zion National Park enables you to prolong your experience and see more of southern Utah's natural beauties and varied landscapes. Each place provides distinct experiences, whether you're climbing among hoodoos at Bryce Canyon or shooting the rocky beauty of Grand Staircase-Escalante.

Chapter Five: Family-Friendly Activities

Hogle Zoo and Tracy Aviary

Hogle Zoo

- **Location:** Salt Lake City, Utah
- **Description:** Hogle Zoo is a family-friendly attraction displaying a varied assortment of species from throughout the globe. Here's what you may expect:
- **Animal Exhibits:** Explore habitats that resemble the natural settings of animals, including elephants, giraffes, large cats, and more.
- **Interactive Experiences:** Enjoy feeding chances, keeper lectures, and educational events throughout the day.
- **Conservation attempts:** Learn about the zoo's conservation programs and attempts to safeguard endangered animals.

- **Special activities:** Check for seasonal activities like BooLights during Halloween and ZooLights throughout the Christmas season.

Tracy Aviary

- **Location:** Liberty Park, Salt Lake City, Utah
- **Description:** Tracy Aviary is a bird sanctuary and educational center with an emphasis on avian conservation and education. Here's what you can explore:
- **Bird Exhibits:** Encounter a wide assortment of bird species from throughout the globe, including rare and endangered species.
- **Interactive Learning:** Participate in educational activities, bird feeding experiences, and aviary tours led by expert personnel.
- **Beautiful Setting:** Enjoy meandering around Liberty Park's serene settings while seeing birds in naturalistic habitats.
- **Events & Activities:** Attend unique events such as bird displays, educational seminars, and seasonal festivities.

Both Hogle Zoo and Tracy Aviary provide fascinating experiences for families, allowing the opportunity to learn about wildlife conservation, engage with animals up close, and enjoy educational events in a gorgeous and family-friendly setting near Salt Lake City, Utah.

Lagoon Amusement Park

- **Location:** Farmington, Utah, near Salt Lake City
- **Description:** Lagoon Amusement Park is a popular family destination with a range of rides, attractions, and entertainment opportunities. Here's what you can anticipate at Lagoon:
- **Rides & Attractions:** Enjoy a combination of thrill rides, family rides, and child rides ideal for all ages. Highlights include roller coasters like Cannibal and Wicked, as well as traditional attractions like the Carousel and Tidal Wave.
- **Waterpark:** Cool off at Lagoon A Beach, a waterpark inside the park with slides, pools, and water play areas suitable for hot summer days.

- **Entertainment:** Catch live concerts, musical performances, and entertainment events throughout the season. Check the schedule for shows at the Lagoon Amphitheater.
- **Games & Arcades:** Play carnival games, try your luck at arcade games, and win prizes at several gaming booths strewn around the park.
- **Dining alternatives:** Choose from several dining alternatives, including restaurants, snack bars, and concession booths providing a range of food and drinks.
- **Seasonal Events:** Experience unique events and holiday festivities, such as Frightmares during the Halloween season and a spectacular Christmas display throughout the winter.
- **Family-Friendly Atmosphere:** Lagoon has something for everyone, whether you're seeking adrenaline-pumping thrills or calm family activities.

Lagoon Amusement Park offers a fun-filled day out for families with activities and entertainment appropriate for all ages, making it a favorite destination for residents and tourists alike in Salt Lake City, Utah.

Museums and Educational Centers

Here are some significant museums and educational facilities in and around Salt Lake City, Utah, that provide engaging experiences for families and visitors:

Museums and Educational Centers in Salt Lake City

Natural History Museum of Utah

- **Description:** Located at the University of Utah, this museum offers exhibits on natural history, including dinosaur fossils, aboriginal civilizations, and the geology of Utah.
- **Highlights:** Interactive displays, the life-size model of a Utahraptor, and spectacular vistas of the Salt Lake Valley from its perch in the foothills.

Clark Planetarium

- **Description:** Offers interactive displays on space exploration, astronomy, and the marvels of the cosmos.

- **Highlights:** Dome theater presentations presenting amazing sights of space, planetarium exhibitions, and hands-on activities for all ages.

Utah Museum of Fine Arts (UMFA)

- **Description:** Located on the University of Utah campus, UMFA displays a broad collection of art from throughout the globe, including European, American, and Asian art.
- **Highlights:** Rotating exhibits, family-friendly art activities, and special events throughout the year.

Discovery Gateway Children's Museum

- **Description:** A hands-on museum in downtown Salt Lake City featuring interactive exhibits and educational events for children.
- **Highlights:** Water play areas, a STEM lab, a garden display, and themed sections like the Kid's Eye View Farm.

The Leonardo Museum

- **Description:** A museum that integrates science, technology, and art with hands-on displays and activities.
- **Highlights:** Exhibits on invention and creativity, seminars, and educational activities centered on science and art.

Red Butte Garden and Arboretum

- **Description:** A botanical garden and research institution linked with the University of Utah, including themed gardens, walking pathways, and seasonal plant exhibits.
- **Highlights:** Children's garden, outdoor concerts, seminars, and family-friendly activities throughout the year.

Educational Centers

- **Loveland Living Planet Aquarium:** Located in Draper, Utah, this aquarium contains marine and freshwater exhibits, interactive touch pools, and educational programs about aquatic life and conservation.

- **Thanksgiving Point:** Located in Lehi, Utah, Thanksgiving Point provides several attractions including the Museum of Ancient Life (dinosaur museum), Butterfly Biosphere, and Ashton Gardens, with themed gardens and seasonal activities.

These museums and educational centers in and around Salt Lake City provide a broad variety of educational and engaging activities for visitors of all ages, making them great locations for families and anyone interested in learning about art, science, history, and the natural world.

Chapter Six: Shopping and Entertainment

Shopping Districts and Malls

Salt Lake City boasts various active retail areas and malls, each with its particular appeal and diversity of businesses. Here are some of the popular retail places in and around Salt Lake City:

Shopping Districts and Malls in Salt Lake City City Creek Center

- **Location:** Downtown Salt Lake City
- **Description:** An upmarket shopping mall providing a combination of high-end boutiques, popular brands, food choices, and entertainment venues. City Creek Center contains both indoor and outdoor retail sections, with picturesque pathways and water elements.
- **Highlights:** Stores including Nordstrom, Macy's, Apple Store, and a range of eateries providing varied cuisines.

The Gateway

- **Location:** Downtown Salt Lake City
- **Description:** An outdoor shopping and entertainment complex recognized for its combination of retail establishments, food choices, and entertainment venues. The Gateway also organizes events, festivals, and concerts throughout the year.
- **Highlights:** Megaplex Theatres, Dave & Buster's, and specialized stores selling unique gifts and local items.

Fashion Place Mall

- **Location:** Murray, Utah (approximately 10 miles south of downtown Salt Lake City)
- **Description:** A vast shopping mall with approximately 100 businesses, including major department stores, fashion merchants, and food choices. Fashion Place Mall provides a pleasant indoor shopping experience with an emphasis on fashion and lifestyle products.

- **Highlights:** Dillard's, Macy's, H&M, Apple Store, and a choice of casual and gourmet eating alternatives.

Trolley Square

- **Location:** Salt Lake City (Historic 600 South & 700 East)
- **Description:** A historic retail mall built in a refurbished trolley barn complex, featuring a mix of specialized stores, boutiques, and eating choices. Trolley Square is recognized for its distinctive architecture and lovely atmosphere.
- **Highlights:** Local shops, specialized businesses, art galleries, and restaurants in a historic urban environment.

Sugar House

- **Location:** Salt Lake City (2100 South & 1100 East)
- **Description:** A stylish area featuring a mix of independent stores, boutiques, cafés, and restaurants. Sugar House provides a more diversified shopping experience with an emphasis on local businesses and unusual items.

- **Highlights:** Sugar House Park adjacent, specialized stores selling vintage apparel, home décor, and **handcrafted items.**

Park City Main Street

- **Location:** Park City, Utah (approximately 30 miles east of downtown Salt Lake City)
- **Description:** A delightful historic street studded with boutiques, galleries, restaurants, and specialized businesses. Park City Main Street provides a unique shopping experience with a mountain resort town vibe.
- **Highlights:** Ski and outdoor gear stores, art galleries, jewelry shops, and eating choices ranging from casual cafes to upscale dining.

These shopping districts and malls in Salt Lake City and neighboring regions offer a variety of opportunities for shopping, eating, and entertainment, appealing to both residents and tourists eager to discover Utah's retail sector.

Art Galleries and Studios

Salt Lake City features a robust arts scene with various art galleries and studios presenting a broad spectrum of creative styles. Here are some noteworthy art galleries and studios to visit in Salt Lake City:

Art Galleries and Studios in Salt Lake City Utah Museum of Fine Arts (UMFA)

- **Description:** Located on the University of Utah campus, UMFA displays a broad collection of art from throughout the globe, including European, American, and Asian art.
- **Highlights:** Rotating exhibits, permanent collections, and educational activities.

Salt Lake Art Center

- **Description:** A contemporary art center concentrating on experimental and inventive artwork by local and international artists.
- **Highlights:** Exhibitions, artist discussions, workshops, and community involvement events.

Modern West Fine Art

- **Description:** Located in downtown Salt Lake City, Modern West Fine Art exhibits modern art with an emphasis on Western landscapes, animals, and area artists.
- **Highlights:** Rotating exhibits, artist receptions, and educational programs.

Art Access Gallery

- **Description:** A nonprofit gallery committed to displaying the work of artists with disabilities and offering accessible art experiences.
- **Highlights:** Exhibitions, community art initiatives, and workshops.

Phillips Gallery

- **Description:** A long-standing gallery in Salt Lake City presenting modern art by local and regional artists.
- **Highlights:** Monthly exhibits, art sales, and a diversity of creative styles and materials.

15th Street Gallery

- **Description:** A modern art gallery in the Sugar House area presents a broad selection of paintings, sculptures, and mixed media artwork.
- **Highlights:** Solo and group exhibits, artist receptions, and art consults.

McKay Gallery

- **Description:** Located at the University of Utah, McKay Gallery showcases exhibits of modern art by students, staff, and visiting artists.
- **Highlights:** Student showcases, faculty exhibits, and public art activities.

These art galleries and studios in Salt Lake City provide different possibilities to study modern and traditional art forms, support local artists, and participate in the lively arts community in Utah's capital city.

Live Music and Theaters

Salt Lake City provides a thriving live music and theatrical culture, with venues ranging from tiny bars to major theaters offering a range of acts. Here are some famous locations to experience live music and theater in Salt Lake City:

Live Music Venues

The Depot

- **Description:** A historic facility situated downtown, recognized for holding performances by national and local musicians across all genres.
- **Highlights:** Intimate atmosphere, full bar, and a broad variety of live music events.

Red Butte Garden Amphitheatre

- **Description:** Located at the University of Utah, this outdoor amphitheater provides summer performances surrounded by stunning gardens and mountain vistas.
- **Highlights:** Acoustic performances, folk, rock, and jazz events, with an emphasis on the outdoor environment.

The State Room

- **Description:** A tiny and intimate venue recognized for its great acoustics and presenting a range of genres, including folk, blues, and indie rock.
- **Highlights:** Seating choices, artisan beverages, and an emphasis on superb sound for live music experiences.

Kilby Court

- **Description:** A tiny, all-ages music venue promoting independent bands and new artists in an intimate atmosphere.
- **Highlights:** DIY environment, reasonable ticket rates, and an emphasis on promoting local and up-and-coming bands.

Theaters & Performing Arts Venues

Eccles Theater

- **Description:** Downtown Salt Lake City's finest location for Broadway musicals, concerts, dance performances, and cultural events.

Highlights: State-of-the-art facilities, vast seating capacity, and a wide program of national touring performances.

Theater Capitol Theatre

- **Description:** A historic theater in downtown Salt Lake City offering ballet performances, opera, Broadway plays, and classical concerts.
- **Highlights:** Ornate architecture, magnificent theater shows, and a cultural monument in the city.

Pioneer Theatre Company

- **Description:** Located at the University of Utah, Pioneer Theatre Company produces professional performances of classic and modern plays and musicals.
- **Highlights:** High-quality performances, skilled cast and crew, and a dedication to theatrical excellence.

Salt Lake Acting Company

- **Description:** A modern theatrical group creating unique and thought-provoking plays and new works.

Highlights: Intimate theater environment, diversified programming, and focus on promoting local talent and writers.

These venues in Salt Lake City provide a rich tapestry of live music and theatrical experiences, catering to a broad variety of preferences and allowing the opportunity to enjoy performances by local, national, and worldwide performers.

Nightlife and Bars

Salt Lake City has a diversified nighttime culture with a mix of pubs, clubs, and entertainment venues catering to all preferences. Here are some popular venues to enjoy nightlife in Salt Lake City:

Nightlife & Bars in Salt Lake City

Bar-X

- **Description:** A traditional cocktail bar noted for its artisan drinks, vintage décor, and intimate setting.

The Ruin

Description: A hip bar providing a large range of craft beers, drinks, and a calm rooftop terrace with views of downtown.

Lake Effect

- **Description:** A large bar and live music venue presenting jazz, blues, and other live acts, along with artisan drinks and a colorful ambiance.

Beer Bar

- **Description:** Known for its large range of local and foreign beers on tap, complemented with gourmet sausages in a relaxed environment.

Gracie's

- **Description:** A bustling pub and restaurant featuring broad food, live music, and a rooftop terrace with views of downtown Salt Lake City.

Sky SLC

- **Description:** A nightclub and event facility featuring DJs, dancing, and a rooftop terrace with panoramic views of the downtown skyline.

Whiskey Street

- **Description:** A whiskey-centric pub featuring a large range of whiskeys, handmade cocktails, and a dynamic ambiance excellent for mingling.

The Bayou

- **Description:** Known for its vast range of over 300 beers, Cajun food, and a vibrant ambiance with live music and outdoor dining.

Entertainment Venues

Wiseguys Comedy Club

- **Description:** Offers stand-up comedy events by local and traveling comedians in a friendly and intimate atmosphere.

Liquid Joe's

- **Description:** A live music venue showcasing rock, metal, and alternative bands, along with DJ nights and themed events.

The Complex

- **Description:** A multi-stage facility featuring concerts, EDM events, and performances by local and national musicians spanning all genres.

Tips for Enjoying Nightlife in Salt Lake City:

- **Check Hours:** Some pubs and clubs may have fixed operation hours owing to local legislation.
- **Plan Ahead:** Consider making reservations, particularly for popular places or over weekends.
- **Dress Code:** Check whether there's a dress code for particular places, including nightclubs and premium pubs.
- **Transit:** Use ridesharing services or public transit to get about safely, particularly if consuming alcoholic drinks.

Salt Lake City's nightlife culture has something for everyone, whether you're wanting to enjoy handmade drinks, live music, or dance the night away in a dynamic setting.

Chapter Seven: Transportation Options

Airports and Airlines

Utah is serviced by many airports, each catering to distinct areas and giving connections to key domestic and international destinations. Here are the key airports in Utah and the airlines that operate from them:

Airports in Utah Salt Lake City International Airport (SLC)

- **Location:** Salt Lake City
- **Description:** The biggest and busiest airport in Utah, acting as a key hub for domestic and international flights.
- **Airlines:** Delta Air Lines, American Airlines, Southwest Airlines, United Airlines, Alaska Airlines, JetBlue Airways, Frontier Airlines, and more.

St. George Regional Airport (SGU)

- **Location:** St. George
- **Description:** Located in southern Utah, servicing the St. George region with flights to and from Salt Lake City and Denver.
- **Airlines:** SkyWest Airlines (running as Delta Connection and United Express).

Provo Airport (PVU)

- **Location:** Provo
- **Description:** A tiny airport servicing the Provo and Utah County region with flights mostly to and from Phoenix-Mesa Gateway Airport.
- **Airlines:** Allegiant Air.

Cedar City Regional Airport (CDC)

- **Location:** Cedar City
- **Description:** Located in southern Utah, servicing the Cedar City area with minimal commercial flights.
- **Airlines:** SkyWest Airlines (running as Delta Connection).

Major Airlines Serving Utah

- **Delta Air Lines:** Operates as a significant airline at Salt Lake City International Airport, operating extensive domestic and some international flights.
- **American Airlines:** Provides domestic flights from Salt Lake City International Airport to several locations around the United States.
- **Southwest Airlines:** Known for its low-cost flights from Salt Lake City International Airport to destinations around the U.S.
- **United Airlines:** Offers domestic and international flights from Salt Lake City International Airport, connecting via key hubs.
- **Alaska Airlines:** Provides flights mostly throughout the West Coast and to select destinations from Salt Lake City International Airport.
- **Frontier Airlines:** Offers budget-friendly flights from Salt Lake City International Airport to several destinations around the U.S.

- **JetBlue Airways:** Operates flights from Salt Lake City International Airport to various locations on the East Coast.

These airports and airlines offer handy alternatives for passengers traveling into and throughout Utah, whether for business, tourism, or connecting to other locations around the United States and abroad.

Car Rentals and Public Transport

In Utah, tourists have access to several transportation alternatives including vehicle rentals and public transit, permitting simple exploration of the state's numerous attractions. Here's a summary of these options:

Car Rentals

Car Rental Companies

- **Description:** Major automobile rental firms operate in Utah, providing a choice of vehicles from tiny cars to SUVs and vans.
- **Availability:** Car rental services are accessible in airports, downtown areas, and major towns like Salt

Lake City, making it easier for visitors to pick up and drop off automobiles.

- **Popular Providers:** Companies like Hertz, Enterprise, Avis, Budget, and National are well-represented throughout the state.

Public Transport

UTA (Utah Transit Authority)

- **Description:** UTA maintains an extensive public transportation network across Utah, including bus, light rail (TRAX), and commuter train (FrontRunner) services.
- **Coverage:** UTA services link major cities and towns like Salt Lake City, Provo, Ogden, and Park City, as well as offering connections to ski resorts during winter months.
- **Convenience:** Routes and timetables are intended to serve both everyday commuters and visitors, with choices for single-ride tickets, day passes, and longer-term passes.

Tips for Getting Around Utah Airport

- **Transfers:** Many automobiles rental firms offer counters at airports for simple pick-up and drop-off.
- **Public Transport Access:** Check UTA's website or mobile app for routes, timetables, and fare information.
- **Seasonal Considerations:** During winter, prepare ahead for road conditions and ski resort transit choices.
- **Explore Regional Diversity:** From national parks to metropolitan hubs, Utah provides different landscapes and attractions accessible via numerous transportations means.

Whether you prefer the freedom of a rental vehicle or the comfort of public transit, Utah's transportation choices adapt to diverse travel tastes and assure smooth exploration of the state's natural beauty and cultural offers.

Road Trip Itineraries

Planning a road trip across Utah provides a rich tapestry of natural marvels, national parks, picturesque roads, and cultural activities. Here are a few interesting road trip itineraries to consider:

Mighty Five National Parks Tour

- **Duration:** 7-10 Days
- **Overview:** Explore Utah's "Mighty Five" national parks, famous for its breathtaking scenery and outdoor activities.

Day 1-2: Salt Lake City to Zion National Park

- Start in Salt Lake City, and discover the city's attractions.
- Drive to Zion National Park (~4 hours).
- Hike Angels Landing or The Narrows, and experience Zion Canyon.

Day 3: Zion to Bryce Canyon National Park

- Drive to Bryce Canyon National Park (~2 hours).
- Witness the hoodoos and climb the Navajo Loop and Queen's Garden Trail.

Day 4: Bryce Canyon to Capitol Reef National Park

- Drive to Capitol Reef National Park (~2.5 hours).
- Explore the gorgeous drive, and trek Capitol Gorge.

Day 5-6: Capitol Reef to Arches National Park

- Drive to Arches National Park (~3 hours).
- Visit Delicate Arch, and Landscape Arch, and climb the Devil's Garden Loop.

Day 7-8: Arches to Canyonlands National Park

- Drive to Canyonlands National Park (Island in the Sky District, ~1.5 hours).
- Enjoy Mesa Arch at dawn, and trek Grand View Point.

Day 9-10: Canyonlands to Salt Lake City

- Drive back to Salt Lake City (~4.5 hours).
- Optional: Visit Dead Horse Point State Park along the way.

Scenic Byways and National Monuments

- **Duration:** 5-7 Days
- **Overview:** Experience Utah's various landscapes and hidden jewels via beautiful byways and national monuments.

Day 1: Salt Lake City to Moab

- Drive to Moab (~3.5 hours).
- Explore Arches National Park and visit Park Avenue, Windows Section.

Day 2: Moab

- Explore Canyonlands National Park (Island in the Sky District).
- Visit Dead Horse Point State Park for sunset.

Day 3: Moab to Monument Valley

- Drive to Monument Valley (~2.5 hours).
- Explore Monument Valley Navajo Tribal Park, and enjoy a guided tour.

Day 4: Monument Valley to Capitol Reef National Park

- Drive to Capitol Reef National Park (~3.5 hours).
- Explore the Waterpocket Fold, and walk Hickman Bridge.

Day 5: Capitol Reef to Salt Lake City

- Drive back to Salt Lake City (~3.5 hours).
- **Optional:** Visit Goblin Valley State Park along the way.

Historic and Cultural Route

- **Duration:** 4-6 Days
- **Overview:** Discover Utah's rich history, cultural sites, and scenic beauty.

Day 1: Salt Lake City

- Explore Temple Square, the Utah State Capitol, and the Natural History Museum of Utah.

Day 2: Salt Lake City to Provo and Park City

- Drive to Provo (~1 hour), see BYU Museum of Art and Provo City Center Temple.

- Drive to Park City (~30 minutes), enjoy Historic Main Street, and see Utah Olympic Park.

Day 3: Park City to Heber Valley and Sundance

- Drive to Heber Valley (~20 minutes), and ride the Heber Valley Railroad.
- Drive to Sundance (~20 minutes), tour Sundance Resort, and climb Stewart Falls.

Day 4: Sundance to Salt Lake City

- Drive back to Salt Lake City (~1 hour).
- **Optional:** Visit Antelope Island State Park for animal watching.

Tips for Road Trips in Utah:

- **Weather Preparedness:** Check weather conditions and road closures, particularly in winter and during the rainy season.
- **Park Passes:** Consider obtaining an America the Beautiful Pass for entrance to national parks and federal recreation grounds.
- **Lodgings:** Book lodgings in advance, particularly during busy seasons and weekends.

- **Safety:** Carry lots of water, food, and a first aid kit, and be careful of animals and park laws.

Utah's road trip alternatives appeal to varied interests, from outdoor adventurers to history aficionados, giving amazing experiences among magnificent landscapes and cultural riches.

Chapter Eight: Accommodations

UTAH HOTELS MAP

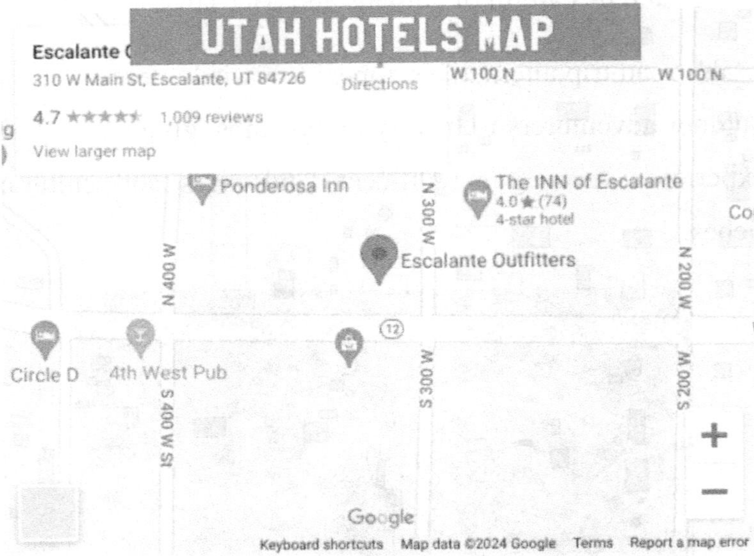

HOW TO SCAN THE QR CODE

- Open your camera app.
- Align the QR code.
- Wait for the prompt.
- Follow the link or action.
- Use a QR code scanner app if necessary

Hotels and Resorts

Utah provides a range of hotels and resorts catering to varied interests, from metropolitan hubs to gorgeous outdoor settings. Here are some significant alternatives around the state:

Hotels & Resorts in Utah

Salt Lake City Area:

- **Grand America Hotel:** A magnificent downtown hotel recognized for its exquisite accommodations, spa facilities, and superb cuisine.
- **Little America Hotel:** Offers pleasant lodgings with features including an outdoor pool, exercise center, and on-site restaurants.

Park City:

- **Stein Eriksen Lodge Deer Valley:** A renowned ski-in/ski-out resort with magnificent accommodations, a full-service spa, and several dining choices.
- **Montage Deer Valley:** Another expensive ski resort boasting big accommodations, ski-in/ski-out access, a huge spa, and multiple restaurants.

Moab:

- **Sorrel River Ranch Resort & Spa:** Located along the Colorado River with luxurious rooms, outdoor activities, and a spa.
- **Red Cliffs Lodge:** Offers rustic charm and breathtaking vistas of the red rock cliffs, along with horseback riding and river rafting.

Zion National Park Area:

- **Zion Lodge:** Situated inside Zion National Park, providing pleasant rooms and convenient access to hiking trails and park activities.
- **Springdale:** Various boutique hotels and lodges near Zion's main gate, allowing quick access to the park's hiking trails and spectacular vistas.

Bryce Canyon National Park Area:

- **Bryce Canyon Lodge:** Located within Bryce Canyon National Park, offers rustic rooms and breathtaking views of the hoodoos.
- **Ruby's Inn:** A popular alternative just outside the park offering a selection of amenities, including hotel rooms, cabins, and RV sites.

Southern Utah (St. George, Cedar City):

- **The Inn at Entrada:** A luxury resort in St. George featuring villa-style rooms, golf courses, and access to outdoor leisure.
- **Abbey Inn & Suites:** Located in Cedar City, offers pleasant accommodations with facilities including a pool, hot tub, and full breakfast.

Tips for Booking Hotels and Resorts in Utah:

- **Book Early:** Especially during busy seasons like summer and ski season, housing may fill up rapidly.
- **Check Location:** Consider closeness to destinations or activities you wish to investigate.
- **Facilities:** Look for resorts or hotels that provide facilities suitable to your interests, such as spa treatments, culinary alternatives, or outdoor activities.
- **Reviews:** Read reviews from other travelers to judge the quality and service of lodgings.

Whether you're seeking a lavish resort experience, a quaint lodge near a national park, or a handy hotel in a city center,

Utah provides a range of alternatives to enrich your stay and exploration of its natural and cultural attractions.

Vacation Rentals

Vacation rentals in Utah give a flexible and typically more intimate accommodation alternative, suitable for families, groups, or those wanting a home-away-from-home experience. Here are some common kinds of vacation rentals and where you may locate them around the state:

Types of Vacation Rentals in Utah

Cabins & Cottages:

- **Description:** Rustic cabins or comfortable cottages are hidden in gorgeous locales, giving seclusion and a close connection to nature.
- **Locations:** Commonly located near national parks like Zion, and Bryce Canyon, and in mountainous places such as Park City and Brian Head.

Vacation Homes & Villas:

- **Description:** Spacious residences or villas with many bedrooms, kitchens, and living spaces, suited for families or bigger groups.

- **Platforms:** Available on vacation rental platforms including Airbnb, Vrbo, and local property management websites.

Condominiums and Apartments:

- **Description:** Condos and apartments with amenities such as kitchens, laundry facilities, and access to communal amenities like pools or fitness centers.
- **Locations:** Found in metropolitan places like Salt Lake City and vacation destinations such as Park City and Moab.

Ski-in/Ski-out Properties:

- **Description:** Properties placed immediately on or near ski slopes, allowing quick access to skiing and snowboarding.
- **Locations:** Ski resorts including Park City Mountain Resort, Deer Valley, and Brian Head.

Lakefront or Riverside Homes:

- **Description:** Homes placed around lakeshores or rivers, allow chances for water activities like boating, fishing, or just enjoying gorgeous views.

- **Locations:** Near lakes such as Bear Lake, and Lake Powell, and along rivers like the Colorado River.

Tips for Booking Vacation Rentals:

- **Book in Advance:** Especially during high seasons or for popular events, vacation homes may fill up rapidly.
- **Read Reviews:** Check reviews from prior guests to judge the quality and dependability of the rental home and host.
- **Check Amenities:** Ensure the rental suits your demands, whether it's WiFi, pet-friendly lodgings, or certain kitchen items.
- **Understand Policies:** Familiarize yourself with cancelation policies, check-in/out hours, and any extra costs or regulations.

Vacation rentals provide a flexible and customized alternative to typical hotels, enabling guests to enjoy Utah's natural beauty and attractions with the conveniences of a home atmosphere.

Bed and Breakfasts

Bed and Breakfasts (B&Bs) in Utah provide a lovely and frequently small overnight experience, merging warm lodgings with personalized service. Here's a glance at what you can anticipate from B&Bs around the state:

Bed & Breakfasts in Utah

Salt Lake City and Surrounding Areas:

- **The Anniversary Inn:** Known for themed rooms and romantic environment, situated in downtown Salt Lake City.
- **Armstrong Home Bed & Breakfast:** A historic home offers magnificent accommodations and near access to attractions like the Utah State Capitol.

Park City:

- **Washington School Inn:** Set in a refurbished schoolhouse, with beautiful accommodations and convenient access to Park City's Main Street and ski areas.
- **The Old Town Guest House:** Overlooking Old Town Park City, offers pleasant accommodations

with mountain views and a short stroll to local stores and eateries.

Moab:

- **Sunflower Hill Inn:** Nestled in a garden setting, giving southwestern charm, an outdoor pool, and convenient access to Arches and Canyonlands National Parks.
- **Cali Shon Boutique Inn:** A boutique-style B&B with creatively furnished rooms, near downtown Moab's restaurants and shopping.

Zion National Park Area:

- **Cliffrose Lodge & Gardens:** Combines B&B charm with resort facilities, situated near the entrance of Zion National Park, giving breathtaking vistas and river access.
- **Canyon Vista Lodge:** Set near Springdale with views of Zion Canyon, giving a calm getaway after visiting the park's trails and vistas.

Bryce Canyon National Park Area:

- **Stone Canyon Inn:** Offering rustic elegance and breathtaking views of Bryce Canyon, including cabins and lodge accommodations with contemporary conveniences.
- **Bryce Canyon Livery Bed & Breakfast:** A historic home with charming accommodations and horseback riding opportunities, near Bryce Canyon's major attractions.

What to Expect at Bed and Breakfasts:

- **Individual Service:** B&Bs generally provide individual service, with hosts giving local advice and suggestions.
- **Homemade Breakfast:** Enjoy a homemade breakfast normally included in your stay, frequently containing local products or specialties.
- **Nice setting:** Experience a nice and intimate setting, especially in historic or particularly themed hotels.
- **Local Charm:** Many B&Bs are housed in historic buildings or gorgeous surroundings, offering a unique view into Utah's culture and environment.

Tips for Booking a Bed and Breakfast:

- **Research:** Read reviews and explore photographs to locate a B&B that suits your tastes and travel style.
- **Check facilities:** Consider what facilities are vital to you, such as WiFi, private baths, or special room characteristics.
- **Book Early:** B&Bs, particularly those near national parks or major tourist locations, may fill up fast, so it's wise to book in advance.

Staying at a Bed & Breakfast in Utah provides a great combination of comfort, warmth, and local character, making it a memorable lodging option for your visit to the Beehive State.

Campgrounds and RV Parks

Utah's various landscapes and outdoor attractions make it a great location for camping and RVing aficionados. Here's a summary of the sorts of campsites and RV parks you may find around the state:

National Park Campgrounds:

- **Description:** Campgrounds inside Utah's national parks provide gorgeous surroundings and convenience to hiking trails and natural attractions.
- **Locations:** Examples include Watchman Campground in Zion National Park, North Campground in Bryce Canyon National Park, and Devils Garden Campground in Arches National Park.

State Park Campgrounds:

- **Description:** Utah's state parks offer a variety of camping alternatives, from established campsites with facilities to more rustic sites for tent camping.
- **Locations:** Popular state park campsites include Dead Horse Point State Park, Goblin Valley State Park, and Kodachrome Basin State Park.

Forest Service Campgrounds:

- **Description:** Managed by the U.S. Forest Service, these campsites are frequently situated in national forests and provide a mix of developed and rustic camping areas.

- **Locations:** Dixie National Forest, Ashley National Forest, and Uinta-Wasatch-Cache National Forest are examples of regions containing Forest Service campsites.

Private Campgrounds and RV Parks:

- **Description:** Privately owned campsites and RV parks provide a variety of services such as full hookups, WiFi, laundry facilities, and recreational activities.
- **Locations:** Found near major locations including Moab, Park City, and along gorgeous highways across Utah.

Bureau of Land Management (BLM) Campgrounds:

- **Description:** BLM-managed lands generally offer scattered camping possibilities and some constructed campsites with limited facilities.
- **Locations:** Particularly prevalent in southern Utah near sites like Moab and Lake Powell, giving magnificent desert vistas and outdoor activity.

Tips for Camping and RVing in Utah:

- **Reservations:** National Park and popular campsite reservations fill up rapidly, particularly during peak seasons. Make reservations in advance if possible.
- **Campground facilities:** Check for facilities such as water, bathrooms, showers, and RV hookups before picking a campground.
- **Permits & Fees:** Be mindful of admission fees, camping fees, and any needed permits for backcountry camping or special activities.
- **Leave No Trace:** Practice Leave No Trace practices to limit influence on natural places, including packing out waste and respecting animals.
- **Weather Preparedness:** Utah's weather may vary considerably based on the season and location. Prepare for hot days, chilly nights, and unpredictable weather fluctuations.

Camping and RVing in Utah give you the chance to immerse yourself in the state's spectacular landscapes and outdoor activities, whether you choose the convenience of an RV park or the rough beauty of a basic campsite.

Chapter Nine: Travel Tips and Essentials

Safety and Health

When going to Utah, ensuring safety and keeping good health are crucial for a nice trip. Here are some safety and health precautions to consider:

Safety Tips

Outdoor Safety:

- **Trekking and Adventure Activities:** Always tell someone of your plan while trekking in rural locations. Carry a map, GPS device, or smartphone with offline maps, and vital supplies including water, food, and a first aid kit.
- **Animal Awareness:** Be mindful of animals such as bears and mountain lions in specific regions. Keep a safe distance and avoid feeding or approaching wild animals.

Driving Safety:

- **Road Conditions:** Utah's different terrain may have variable road conditions. Check weather predictions and road conditions, particularly during winter, and drive carefully.
- **Seatbelt Use:** Ensure everyone in the car wears seatbelts. Utah law requires all passengers to be properly restrained.

Weather Preparedness:

- **Heat and Sun Protection:** Utah's desert areas may endure extreme temperatures. Stay hydrated, use sunscreen, and seek shade during high solar hours.
- **Winter Safety:** If traveling in winter, be prepared for snow and slippery conditions. Equip your vehicle with winter tires or chains, and drive cautiously on snow-covered roads.

Emergency Contacts:

- **Know Local Emergency Numbers:** Keep a list of local emergency numbers, including police, fire, and medical agencies.

- **Cell Phone service:** In distant places, cell phone service may be restricted. Plan properly and bring backup communication devices if required.

Health Tips

Altitude Considerations:

High Altitude Areas: Some regions of Utah, such as ski resorts and national parks, are at high elevations. Take time to acclimate if going from lower altitudes, and drink lots of fluids to avoid altitude sickness.

Hydration and Nutrition:

- **Water Intake:** Stay hydrated, particularly in Utah's arid environment. Carry water bottles and replenish them often, especially during outdoor activities.
- **Healthy Eating:** Enjoy local food but also keep a balanced diet. Seek fresh fruits and vegetables to complement your meals.

Medical Facilities:

- **Healthcare Services:** Locate nearest hospitals, clinics, or urgent care facilities along your trip path. Carry required medicines and a copy of prescriptions if needed.
- **Travel Insurance:** Consider travel insurance that covers medical emergencies and evacuation, particularly for outdoor activities or isolated regions.

By emphasizing safety precautions and health concerns, you may enjoy your vacation to Utah while discovering its natural beauty and cultural attractions with peace of mind.

Packing Lists

Packing for a vacation to Utah should reflect the varied activities and temperatures you can experience, whether touring national parks, skiing, or visiting cultural sites. Here are key things to include in your packing list:

Essential Packing List for Utah

Clothing:

- **Comfortable Walking Shoes:** Sturdy hiking boots or walking shoes for outdoor activities.

- **Layered apparel:** Lightweight and breathable apparel for warm days and chilly nights.
- **Warm Layers:** Fleece jacket or sweater for colder weather, particularly in higher altitudes.
- **Rain Jacket or Poncho:** Waterproof or water-resistant jacket for unexpected rain showers.
- **Hat and Sunglasses:** Sun protection is needed, particularly in Utah's bright environment.
- **Swimsuit:** If going to visit hot springs or lakes during summer months.

Gear and Accessories:

- **Daypack or Backpack:** For carrying water, food, and supplies on treks and day trips.
- **Reusable Water Bottle:** Stay hydrated with a sturdy water bottle that can be refilled throughout the day.
- **Sunscreen and Lip Balm:** High SPF sunscreen and lip balm with UV protection for sun-exposed activities.
- **Camera or Smartphone:** Capture amazing moments of Utah's scenery and attractions.

- **Binoculars:** For birding or observing distant vistas in national parks.

Health and Safety:

- **First Aid Kit:** Basic items such as bandages, antiseptic wipes, pain relievers, and any personal prescriptions.
- **Hand Sanitizer:** Carry travel-sized hand sanitizer for cleaning during outdoor activities.
- **Personal Identification and Health Insurance Card:** Keep these crucial papers in a safe location.
- **Emergency Contacts:** List of local emergency numbers and contacts for your trip.

Electronics and Miscellaneous:

- **Chargers:** Pack chargers for your equipment, including cellphones, cameras, and other devices.
- **Travel adaptor:** If you're going from overseas, verify you have the right adaptor for U.S. electrical outlets.
- **Travel Guide or Maps:** Physical or digital maps of Utah's regions and attractions.

- Travel Locks: Secure your bags and items during transportation and hotel stays.

Optional Items:

- **Binoculars:** For wildlife watching and picturesque lookouts.
- **Outdoor Gear:** Depending on activity, consider packing hiking poles, camping gear, or ski equipment if traveling in winter.
- **Reusable Bags:** Eco-friendly bags for shopping or transporting souvenirs.

Tips for Packing:

- **Check Weather Forecasts:** Utah's weather may vary by place and season. Pack appropriately, particularly for chilly evenings or high-altitude excursions.
- **Pack Light:** Opt for adaptable apparel and basics that may be layered or mix-and-matched for varied activities.
- **Plan for Outside Activities:** Include items suited to your intended outside trips, such as hiking boots, daypacks, or ski apparel.

By packing carefully and considering the activities and temperatures you'll experience, you'll be well-prepared to enjoy Utah's gorgeous scenery and numerous attractions to the fullest.

Local Etiquette

When visiting Utah, recognizing and observing local etiquette may improve your experience and relationships with inhabitants. Here are some crucial etiquette guidelines to bear in mind:

Local Etiquette in Utah

Respect for Religious Customs:

- **Mormon Influence:** Utah has a significant cultural and historical link to The Church of Jesus Christ of Latter-day Saints (LDS Church). While not everyone in Utah is Mormon, be aware that many inhabitants subscribe to LDS beliefs and practices.
- **Places of Worship:** If visiting religious places like temples or churches, dress modestly and obey any set regulations or rituals.

Courtesy and Politeness:

- **Friendly Interactions:** Utahns are often noted for their friendliness and hospitality. Greet individuals with a smile and be respectful in public encounters.
- **Thank You:** Express thankfulness with a simple "thank you" or "thanks."

Tipping and Service Expectations:

- **Tipping:** In restaurants and for services like cabs or hair salons, tipping is typical. Standard tipping rates in the U.S. vary from 15% to 20% of the entire cost.
- **Service Standards:** Expect fast and polite service at restaurants and shops.

Outdoor Etiquette:

- **Leave No Trace:** When visiting Utah's natural regions, adopt Leave No Trace principles. Pack out all litter, remain on authorized routes, and respect animals and vegetation.
- **Sharing Trails:** Yield to walkers heading uphill, while bicycles yield to both hikers and equestrians.

Alcohol Laws:

- **Utah's regulations:** Utah has unique alcohol regulations compared to other states. Alcoholic drinks are controlled, and certain locations may have limits on alcohol sales or usage. Familiarize oneself with local restrictions if going to consume alcohol.

Cultural Sensitivity:

- **Diversified Community:** Utah is growing more diversified with a variety of ethnicities and backgrounds. Respect cultural diversity and avoid making judgments about others based on appearance or background.

Driving and Transportation:

- **Road Courtesy:** Follow traffic regulations, defer to pedestrians, and use turn signals when changing lanes.
- **Public Transport:** If using public transportation, follow quiet zones and give up seats to elderly or handicapped people when appropriate.

Social Conversations:

- **Topics of Discussion:** Conversations about outdoor activities, local attractions, and family are frequently safe topics. Avoid delicate or contentious subjects unless stated by your local host.

Environmental Stewardship:

- **Respect Nature:** Utahns cherish their natural surroundings. Avoid trash, respect animals, and stick to park restrictions while visiting outdoor areas.

By being attentive to local traditions and demonstrating respect for Utah's cultural and natural history, you'll contribute to a good and memorable experience for yourself and others you meet throughout your stay.

Chapter Ten: Itineraries

3-Day Itinerary

Here's a proposed 3-day schedule to visit some of Utah's attractions, mixing outdoor experiences, gorgeous landscapes, and cultural exploration:

Day 1: Salt Lake City Exploration

- **Morning:** Start your day with a visit to Temple Square, enjoying the gardens and ancient structures.
- **Late Morning:** Visit the Utah State Capitol for panoramic views of the city and learn about Utah's history.
- **Lunch:** Enjoy a lunch at a local downtown restaurant, recognized for its wide food selections.
- **Afternoon:** Explore the Natural History Museum of Utah or take a walk around the Red Butte Garden and Arboretum.
- **Evening:** Dine at a restaurant along Main Street or in the downtown area, savoring Salt Lake City's culinary culture.

Day 2: Park City and Outdoor Adventure

- **Morning:** Drive to Park City (approximately 30 minutes from Salt Lake City).
- **Late Morning:** Explore Park City's historic Main Street, noted for its galleries, shops, and eateries.
- **Lunch:** Enjoy lunch at a café or restaurant in Park City.
- **Afternoon:** Visit Utah Olympic Park to learn about the 2002 Winter Olympics and see competitor's train.
- **Late Afternoon:** If coming in winter, enjoy skiing or snowboarding at Park City Mountain Resort or Deer Valley Resort. In summer, explore hiking or mountain biking paths.
- **Evening:** Relax with supper in Park City and consider attending a cultural event or live music performance.

Day 3: Outdoor Adventure in Moab

- **Morning:** Drive to Moab (approximately 3.5 hours from Salt Lake City).

- **Late Morning:** Visit Arches National Park and climb renowned monuments like Delicate Arch or Landscape Arch.
- **Lunch:** Have a picnic lunch in the park or eat at a restaurant in Moab.
- **Afternoon:** Explore Canyonlands National Park, concentrating on the Island in the Sky section and overlooks like Mesa Arch or Grand View Point.
- **Late Afternoon:** Optionally, enjoy outdoor activities such as river rafting on the Colorado River or a spectacular fly above the parks.
- **Evening:** Return to Moab for supper and unwind after a day of outdoor activity.

Tips for Your Itinerary:

- **Travel Considerations:** Plan for travel times between places and verify park hours and trail conditions in advance.
- **Packing Essentials:** Bring comfortable walking shoes, sunscreen, and lots of water for outdoor activities.

- **Bookings:** Make bookings for hotels and popular activities ahead of time, particularly during peak seasons.
- **Flexibility:** Adjust the plan depending on your interests and the local advice you obtain throughout your stay.

This schedule enables you to enjoy a combination of Utah's urban culture in Salt Lake City, outdoor experiences in Park City, and the spectacular natural splendor of Moab's national parks in only three days. Adjustments may be made depending on your preferences and the time of year you want to visit.

7-Day Itinerary

Here's a detailed 7-day plan to tour the different landscapes, national parks, and cultural sites of Utah:

Day 1: Arrival in Salt Lake City

- **Arrival:** Arrive in Salt Lake City, Utah.
- **Explore Downtown:** Visit Temple Square, Utah State Capitol, and eat supper in downtown Salt Lake City.

Day 2: Salt Lake City to Park City

- **Morning:** Drive to Park City (approximately 30 minutes from Salt Lake City).
- **Historic Main Street:** Explore Park City's Historic Main Street, explore galleries, and boutiques, and have lunch.
- **Outdoor Activities:** Visit Utah Olympic Park for activities like zip-lining or the Alpine Slide.
- **Evening:** Relax and eat in Park City.

Day 3: Park City to Moab

- **Morning:** Depart early for Moab (approximately 4 hours driving).
- **Arches National Park:** Explore Arches National Park, trek to Delicate Arch, and view other iconic arches.
- **Evening:** Overnight in Moab, supper in town.

Day 4: Moab - Canyonlands National Park

- **Morning:** Visit Canyonlands National Park, Island in the Sky area. Enjoy magnificent viewpoints including Mesa Arch and Grand View Point.

- **Afternoon:** Optional options include hiking or a guided tour.
- **Evening:** Return to Moab, supper, and rest.

Day 5: Moab - Dead Horse Point State Park & Scenic Drive

- **Morning:** Visit Dead Horse Point State Park for spectacular views of the Colorado River.
- **Picturesque Drive:** Drive the picturesque road along Highway 128 near the Colorado River.
- **Afternoon:** Optional activities include river rafting or viewing local art galleries.
- **Evening:** Dinner in Moab.

Day 6: Moab to Capitol Reef National Park

- **Morning:** Drive to Capitol Reef National Park (approximately 2.5 hours).
- **Picturesque road:** Explore the park's picturesque road and stop at views.
- **Hiking:** Hike through Capitol Gorge or other paths.
- **Evening:** Stay overnight in Torrey or nearby, supper in the neighborhood.

Day 7: Capitol Reef to Salt Lake City

- **Morning:** Visit more of Capitol Reef, and possibly discover old orchards or petroglyphs.
- **Afternoon:** Return to Salt Lake City (approximately 3.5 hours driving).
- **Evening:** Final meal in Salt Lake City, enjoy local entertainment or sights.

Tips for Your Itinerary:

- **National Park Pass:** Consider obtaining a National Places Pass if visiting numerous places.
- **Reservations:** Book lodgings and activities in advance, particularly during high seasons.
- **Weather:** Check weather conditions and prepare appropriately, particularly for outdoor activities.

Flexibility: Be prepared to change plans depending on weather conditions or unexpected closures.

This program provides a combination of urban experience in Salt Lake City, outdoor activity in national parks, and picturesque drives across Utah's gorgeous landscapes.

Adjustments may be made depending on your interests and available time. Enjoy your tour of Utah!

Two-Week Itinerary

For a complete two-week plan in Utah, you may see a greater choice of national parks, scenic drives, outdoor activities, and cultural landmarks. Here's a thorough strategy to make the most of your time:

Day 1-2: Salt Lake City

- **Day 1:** Arrival in Salt Lake City. Explore Temple Square, the Utah State Capitol, and downtown attractions.
- Day 2: Visit the Natural History Museum of Utah, Red Butte Garden, or enjoy outdoor activities around the city.

Day 3-4: Park City and Surroundings

- Day 3: Drive to Park City. Explore Historic Main Street, Utah Olympic Park events, and neighborhood galleries.

- Day 4: Outdoor activity in Park City: skiing (winter) or hiking/biking (summer). Optional travel to adjacent communities like Heber City or Midway.

Day 5-6: Moab - Arches and Canyonlands National Parks

- **Day 5:** Drive to Moab (approximately 4 hours). Visit Arches National Park and trek to Delicate Arch and other monuments.
- **Day 6:** Explore Canyonlands National Park (Island in the Sky section). Optional activities include river rafting or guided excursions in Moab.

Day 7-8: Moab - Dead Horse Point and Scenic Drives

- **Day 7:** Visit Dead Horse Point State Park for panoramic views of the Colorado River. Drive along Highway 128 for magnificent scenery.
- **Day 8:** Explore more of Moab or neighboring attractions like the La Sal Mountains or local art galleries.

Day 9-10: Capitol Reef National Park

- **Day 9:** Drive to Capitol Reef National Park (approximately 2.5 hours). Explore picturesque highways, and historic orchards, and climb Capitol Gorge.
- **Day 10:** Visit the Capitol Reef Visitor Center, climb other trails, or visit adjacent communities like Torrey.

Day 11-12: Bryce Canyon National Park

- **Day 11:** Drive to Bryce Canyon National Park (approximately 2 hours). Explore the amphitheaters, and trek routes like Navajo Loop or Queen's Garden.
- **Day 12:** Sunrise at Bryce Canyon. Optional activities include horseback riding, astronomy excursions, or visiting adjacent Dixie National Forest.

Day 13-14: Zion National Park

- **Day 13:** Drive to Zion National Park (approximately 2 hours). Hike renowned paths like Angel's Landing or The Narrows.

- **Day 14:** Explore more of Zion: explore Zion Canyon's beautiful Drive, and Emerald Pools, or enjoy a beautiful drive around the park.

Day 15: Return to Salt Lake City

- **Morning:** Drive back to Salt Lake City (approximately 4-5 hours). Optionally, stop at Cedar Breaks National Monument or other lovely locations along the road.
- **Afternoon:** Return rental vehicles, and check into a motel in Salt Lake City.
- Evening: Farewell supper in Salt Lake City, reminiscing on your Utah experience.

Tips for Your Itinerary:

- **Park Passes:** Consider obtaining an America the Beautiful Pass or individual park passes ahead of time.
- **Lodgings:** Book lodgings in advance, particularly during busy seasons and near national parks.
- **Activities:** Research and arrange activities like guided tours, ranger programs, or outdoor rentals early, particularly for popular activities.

Weather: Check weather predictions and prepare appropriately, particularly for outdoor activities and diverse climes.

This two-week itinerary provides a complete overview of Utah's national parks, outdoor activities, and cultural landmarks, delivering a remarkable experience across the different landscapes of the Beehive State. Adjustments might be made depending on personal interests and travel preferences.

Made in the USA
Monee, IL
03 October 2024

67118475R00075